The Reflection Series
Daily reflection for graceful difference in a negative world.

A 7-day study… give God a week.

BOLD GOOD

Dawn Marion Hudgins

BOLD GOOD
The Reflection Series:
Daily reflection for graceful difference in a negative world.

Copyright © 2018 by Dawn Marion Hudgins
All rights reserved.

International Standard Book Number: 978-1717163523

Printed in the United States of America

Inspiration of
BOLD GOOD

The inspiration for this REFLECTIVE STUDY, was revealed in a line of one of my husband's sermons... *'the world is loud with evil and negativity, we need to be the BOLD GOOD.'*

Although I am not the BOLD GOOD, it is the desire of my heart, and therefore a continuous work of striving toward this goal. To do this, I must know who I am, recognize who I want to be, listen to God, and search his guidance through His word and strive toward this daily.

*"The world is loud with evil and negativity, we need to be the **BOLD GOOD**."*

Rev. Ron Hayes

CONTENTS

Day 1: Let Go and Let Him

Day 2: Permission to Be Different

Day 3: Judgement Free Zone

Day 4: It's a Social Media World – Choose Carefully

Day 5: Be There

Day 6: The Gospel according to you? Or God?

Day 7: Careful HOW you say it

ONE

LET GO and Let Him

And I am sure of this, that he who began a good work in you will bring it to completion at the day of Jesus Christ.
Philippians 1:6

OVERVIEW
When we spend too much time in self-ridicule, we distance ourselves from Christ and from others. It is hard to see others, help others, when we are focused on ourselves.

We can be our own worst critics. We look in the mirror and we see ourselves through a microscope that no one else can see and the magnification is multiplied. Our minds fill with a thought, a series of thoughts, that then apply weight to our feelings. It can start as something small. If this goes on for multiple days, it becomes a habit, and then it becomes who we are.

Whether it is thoughts about ourselves, about others, or about life in general, it is important to find God's blessings, even in the midst of a mighty storm. And I know firsthand that there are somedays were this might be near impossible.

Our minds, our 'who we are', need to be fed just as our bellies. When we fill our bellies with the things that are good for growth, we experience positive growth. When we feed ourselves with things that aren't so good for us, what happens? We gain weight, our blood pressure increases, our cholesterol gets higher, we become sluggish and we become unhealthy. When we listen to music that has toxic lyrics, slow BPM (Beats Per Minute), and anxious composition, it clouds our minds. Neurologically there are chemical changes that occur within our brains that increase depression, anger, and negativity. If we stay in this state for too long, we too change... and not for the better.

Being one who tends to spend too much time in my own head, this is a constant battle for me. But the good news is there are ways to combat this. Your playlist is one. Yep, your playlist.

Playlist Challenge:
Work with me here, I promise that this is all scientifically documented 😊. I challenge you, for one week, to listen to music that ONLY
1. has beats that are between 120 and 140 BPM (Beats Per Minute)
2. has positive lyrics

Why? We are going to train your brain. When you listen to positive lyrics to songs where the BPM is between 120 and 140 something truly amazing happens in your brain. It excretes perfect levels of Norepinephrine, Serotonin, and Dopamine while lowering your levels of cortisol. What does this mean you ask? Well, antidepressants mimic the release of these chemicals in your brain. Only music does it naturally. Now, I am no doctor, I do not play one on TV and am not prescribing 'instead of', that is between you and your physician. However, MRI's have shown that when you listen to this type of music, it releases these chemicals in such a way that it will actually change your mood... positively. It will boost self-confidence, reduce fatigue, it can increase your endurance when you exercise, it even makes you tap your foot. Music is a powerful gift from God. There are other things music can do to improve your life as well, but that is information in another book. To move the challenge further, I recommend the music to be God inspired. Your choice on who sings. My personal playlist consists of I AM THEY, Casting Crowns, Third Day, and more. (It even contains bluegrass, because you can't stay in a bad mood and listen to bluegrass, the music won't let you.)

Do this for a week. It will take a little preparation. In addition to changing your playlist, remove yourself from mood altering altercations. If there is someone in your life who is extremely negative, give that relationship a break for a week. Allow yourself time to heal and get stronger.

Also, one last thing... when you look in the mirror in the morning and you find yourself saying something negative about yourself... STOP... and say something positive, and even if you don't feel like it, smile, SMILE BIG...laugh out loud till the laughter becomes real.

Actively do this, and I tell you, you will be surprised at how different you feel at the end of the week.

So, LET GO. Give yourself permission to let go of the negativity. Let go of the negative thoughts about yourself. Let go of the heaviness in your life that weighs you down. God is good. He has begun a work in you, and He will finish it. He loves you as if YOU are the only one. He knows your thoughts, your dreams, your desires, HE knows what is best for you.

When we start feeling a little better about ourselves, and we work outside of ourselves with others, share our improvements that we have made within ourselves, we can see the hurt and the need of others. We can reach out to them and help them. We can be the BOLD GOOD in a quiet way. Your health, your struggles, your realness, are a testimony to encourage and strengthen others. Never forget that. God shapes us and stretches us to meet His path for us and as He stretches and shapes us, there can be growing pains, but He is always there seeing us through. He is our biggest encourager. So, Let Go, of all that is keeping you from being a better you and Let God mold you. He knows exactly what you need, and WHEN you need it.

REFLECTION:

I challenge you to pray today for God to show you opportunity to love yourself, to extend forgiveness, to seek His will. I challenge you to complete the playlist challenge. It will change you, it will guide you on a road to a better you.

TWO

Permission to be
DIFFERENT

But even the hairs of your head are all numbered.
Matthew 10:30

OVERVIEW
We are all different.
God made us that way... with Planned Purpose.

Years ago, when I use to do a lot of public speaking and motivational training, I loved using the analogy and quote from Albert Einstein of the fish and the tree. You know the one,

"Everybody is a genius. But if you judge a fish by its ability to climb a tree, it will live its whole life believing that it is stupid."

Diversity is a wonderful thing. You will hear me say this over and over again. I have truly great opportunities in my life that have allowed me to meet people from all over the world. Having said that, I truly consider many of them as close friends and they are wonderful people. They are also very different from me.

I spent the majority of my childhood, teenage years and yes even adult hood thinking there was something wrong with me. I knew God loved me. I knew I shouldn't feel this way, but I did. I always felt inferior to others because I thought differently. I always felt judged by others because I was, in my opinion, different. Truth be told, maybe they did judge me. Maybe I am not as odd, weird, or strange as I have always thought myself to be. Maybe I am. What I do know is that God made me, just the way I am to fulfil the purpose He has set for me.

Of all the historical figures in the Bible, I identify most closely with David, yep, David. There are many reasons for this, and if you ever want to know the entire story we can chat over a cup of tea. However, for today's purpose it is regarding his 'fit' ness. There are lots of things about David to discuss but let's focus just on the battle with the Philistines. David, although not very old, was the BOLD GOOD that day. He was confident God was with him. He was certain God would see him through. He was fearless with his slinging abilities. As a child I heard the story of David and Goliath as the underdog prevailing. As an adult I see the story entirely different. Goliath was the underdog. Yes, it is true he was bigger, had more experience as a warrior, and had great armor. In contrast, David, with no armor, with smaller stature, had something else. He had the knowledge, skill, technique, confidence, and preparation. He had already slayed a bear and a lion. God had prepared him for this moment. He had experienced perfect practice. He was proven at his skill and talent, and to top it all off, God was with him. God didn't just stick him in a situation unprepared. He had been thoroughly prepped for this. He was a skilled assassin with his sling. Scientists have calculated that the velocity of the Barium Sulfate rock slung from his sling had the same impact as that of a .45 caliber bullet. Yep, Goliath was the underdog. David was different than other men, and God prepared him, stretched him, and shaped him for every situation he encountered.

IT IS OK THAT I AM DIFFERENT. It is ok, because my purpose is different than yours. God's plan for me is different than yours and it takes ALL of us to be the body of Christ.

Instead of pointing out nicks and kinks in the armor of our fellow man, let's rejoice in our differences. Let's learn more about what we don't understand in a loving way. Ask questions. Be interested. Get invested in the lives of others. Encourage, support, love one another.

Another favorite quote of mine is from politician Dudley Malone (American Politician 1882-1950)

> *"I've never in my life learned anything from any man who agreed with me."*

We need to give ourselves PERMISSION to be different.

It's really ok, to not be ok, or to be amazing. God's has a 'fit'ness plan for each of us.

REFLECTION:

"Indeed, the very hairs of your head are all numbered. Don't be afraid; you are worth more than many sparrows."
Luke 12:7

I wouldn't want to see the schematic, that is my head of hair. That would be overwhelming but think about that. Each one of our hairs is numbered. This probably even takes into account the ones we shed on the shower floor each day. This connects me back to Psalms 139. Although the entire passage is a testament to our individuality and how God knows us completely, in verses 15 – 16 it is written:

My frame was not hidden from you when I was made in the secret place, when I was woven together in the depths of the earth. Your eyes saw my unformed body; all the days ordained for me were written in your book before one of them came to be.

God knows us. He is preparing us to be just as we should be. We are not a mistake, but a carefully planned, loved, supported instrument of His. Each of us. So, give your brother a break and allow them to be who God is preparing. If they haven't found His way yet, pray for them, encourage them, show them love. Allow God to do His work in them. He's got this.

THREE

Judgement Free Zone

Judge not, that you be not judged. For with the judgment you pronounce you will be judged, and with the measure you use it will be measured to you. Why do you see the speck that is in your brother's eye, but do not notice the log that is in your own eye? Or how can you say to your brother, 'Let me take the speck out of your eye,' when there is the log in your own eye? You hypocrite, first take the log out of your own eye, and then you will see clearly to take the speck out of your brother's eye.

Matthew 7:1-29

OVERVIEW:

JUDGEMENT AND LOVE CANNOT OCCUPY THE SAME SPACE.

I remember hearing about a pastor who preached the same sermon six weeks in a row. On the sixth Sunday, a congregant came up to him and said, 'Pastor, that's two weeks in a row you've preached that sermon, I think we've got it now.'

I don't know about you, but I am slow enough where I need to hear certain messages numerous times before they sink into my thick skull and take root. I am a slow learner that needs constant reminding.

A few years ago, I was working with someone on their wedding. This person was normally very practical, thorough in thought, not flashy, simple, sensible, ... pragmatic. Her wedding on the other hand, did not resemble the person I knew at all. The photography team was like that of a paparazzi. Her dress was from a top designer. Her hair was perfectly styled with new color, curls, and accoutrement. The event took place at the country club with the finest of everything. Although the photographs were amazing, and truly looked as if they were ripped right from the pages of Metropolitan magazine, they looked almost nothing like the bride. Normally she did not color her hair, it was usually straight, usually 2 days from a washing, no make-up, sweatshirts, sweatpants, sneakers and comfort. She was normally very simplistic. However, on this day, the day where the photographs have now shown up for every occasion for three years on social media are of this person, whom looks and acts nothing like the one I know.

I know that this is not unusual.

**We are cultivating a
FACEGRAM, INSTACHAT, CHATBOOK,
life, that doesn't resemble reality.**

The danger of this, is that we begin comparing our 'real' life, with the 'perceived' life of others. We don't see the bags under their eyes, or the massive bill associated with the event that will take months to payoff, or the relationship that went sour because of the 'need to be perceived' a certain way. We don't see the ugliness. We assume... that these photographs are the total picture instead of a momentary snapshot into their lives. We compare ourselves to this and in ourselves, cultivate uncertainness, depression, negativity, etc.

Sometimes these people ARE happy. Sometimes, they are NOT.

The truth is we are always in one of three places:
    1. We have either just come out of a valley
    2. We are going into a valley, or
    3. We are presently in the depths of the valley

Do we stop to *really* look at others and see where they are? See the truth? Do we feel the truth and listen to their words? Most importantly, do we listen to their heart?
Judgement build walls. Judgment separates. It does not unify or build or heal.

I was once told that there are 3 sides to every story; mine, yours, and the factual way it actually is. We base our opinions on our emotions, on our experiences, on our value system, on our cultures and our developed beliefs. And we apply weight to them, giving them hierarchy over the thoughts and values of others.

As Christians, we strive to live by a certain standard. Following in the footsteps of Christ. We fall, we stumble, we fail, but sometimes we do good, give back, help others, and share the love of Christ. Our goal should be to do this with every action. That we strive to be a constant humble example of the love that Jesus showed throughout His ministry and the grace He still shows today. If I am working to get closer to Christ... if I am working toward sharing his love with others... if

I am working on my humility, humanness, and striving for a closer relationship, there is only room for love. There is no need to pretend to be something we are not. After all, I am human, we are all human. We all fail, we all succeed. Sometimes our greatest witness could be how we handle failure or in sharing how we feel, think, live, and learn.

Our lives shouldn't be an embellishment of the truth on **FACEGRAM, INSTACHAT, and CHATBOOK.**

I'm not saying air everything on these channels, far from it. It is a good habit to NOT AIR YOUR DIRTY LAUNDRY, in any way.

What I am suggesting is, that *you* are real. Don't assume the posts you see are accurate. They might be. They might also be an illusion of what the poster wants them to be. Our judgement, our evaluation of their lives compared to our beliefs or how we would handle situations, does not bridge, it separates.

REFLECTION:
Since LOVE and JUDGEMENT cannot occupy the same space. Choose love. Seek the truth and see the opportunity to share the love of Christ. Do not practice judgement. If a thought passes your mind that is judging and comparing how you would do verses how they would do, stop yourself and realign. Your standards, your thoughts, your life, is not theirs. You did not come from the same place or perspective. You may not share the same demons. You do not share the same past, but if by chance, when you are looking to really see them, you see that you do share the same demons, you have an opportunity to support and love them and

in return you will grow too. It is an opportunity to be the GOOD. The Bold Good.

FOUR

It's a
Social Media World...
Choose Carefully

... present your bodies as a living sacrifice, holy and acceptable to God, which is your spiritual worship. Do not be conformed to this world, but be transformed by the renewal of your mind, that by testing you may discern what is the will of God, what is good and acceptable and perfect. For by the grace given to me I say to everyone among you not to think of himself more highly than he ought to think, but to think with sober judgment, each according to the measure of faith that God has assigned. For as in one body we have many members, and the members do not all have the same function, so we, though many, are one body in Christ, and individually members one of another. ...

Romans 12: 1-21

Overview
Choose responses and posts with point and purpose, always knowing that every word is an opportunity to lift-up the Lord Jesus Christ. Equally it is an opportunity to quickly destroy your witness and add yourself to the vast wasteland of those who claim Christ, but do not act with love, grace, mercy or understanding. This gives Christianity a bad name, and it pushes many further from God.

I would have to say that there are many things I love about social media. I can see quickly photos of friends and their families, know what is going on in their lives, get updates on the news (even though I realize this shouldn't be my news outlet), invite others to events, or be invited to events, see where the hurt is in our community - add them to my prayer list, and much more. However, on the flip side, there are a few things about social media I detest. The political season has to be my most hated time on Facebook. I am amazed at the bashing that takes place between parties and against friends. It becomes a forum for judgement, ridicule, falsities, and hatred. It brings out the evil that is within us.

With that statement, 'the evil that is within us', I am reminded of scripture that you will hear me mention with some regularity. It is part of my personal arsenal, an arrow in my quiver, Ephesians 6:10-18. But we will come to that later this week. Today, I want you to reflect upon Romans 12:1–21. *'Do not be conformed to this world.'* This world is a diverse place and I do love diversity.

When it comes to diversity, there are so many things to learn and understand about others and their cultures, but additionally, it lends itself to a multitude of ideas, practices, falsities, and sway. False sway is a thorn for me. These are the ideas that some believe so firmly in, but they have no root of fact or proof, and unfortunately, we have entered into a climate where if you do not believe the way I do, you are grossly wrong. These false beliefs have been cultivated by experience, an insertion of thought from satan (satan, in my opinion, doesn't deserve to have his name capitalized) himself and sometimes strong conversations of persuasion, that in turn are manifested into what we believe as fact, but truly has no factual basis. Then we turn and post them; ridicule and criticize others for not believing the way that we do. Almost as if their opinion is wrong unless it aligns with our own.

Analyzing these actions takes far too much energy. Responding in negativity, alienates us from our purpose.

So, should we respond?

No doubt these situations can bring strong emotion, and often encourage us to lash out. So, if we choose to respond, how do we do it in such a way that still is uplifting to Christ? How do we do it in a way that doesn't alienate? How do we properly approach different opinions from ours, and how do we approach those whom light a fire of anger within us based on their comments?

Recently a former classmate of mine posted on Facebook that he is tired of having Christians shove their beliefs down his throat. Now, I must say, I have no idea who he is hanging out with, nor do I know all of his friends on Facebook. Here is what I do know… He feels strongly about this. He additionally feels strongly that there is a strong hypocritical presence from these people.

As a Baptist, I have often been told, *'you're not a Baptist, you don't believe what they do'*. The first couple of times I heard this it caused my head to turn, my eye brows to raise, and the question crossed my lips, *'What is it that you think I believe?'* I was amazed at what I heard Baptist's believe. In his eyes we are close minded, have no tolerance for the LGBTQ community, drink and cheat on our spouses behind closed doors and ridicule those who do it openly, and his list went on. I was at first happy to know he didn't put me in this classification, but then I was a bit confused and hurt that he believed all Baptist feel this way.

FYI:
ALL, NEVER, ALWAYS, EVERYONE, ETC.
THESE ARE WORDS WE SHOULD <u>NOT</u> USE.
THEY ARE DIVICIVE AND UNTRUE.

Of course, I will not deny that there might be some out there who do. I will not speak for them, but I do know many who do not hold these beliefs. So, where is he getting this from? In writing this I decided to google a well-known outspoken Baptist church, and I was saddened to see what came up in my first pass. It was a big pile of hatred. It is no wonder there are some who are turned-off by Christianity when the values of hatred are spewed.

So, what can we do?

Fundamentally, I will always say, *Know What You Believe* and in saying this, *Does What You Believe Align with the Bible?* Not, *does it align with religion*, but *does it align with the Bible?*

In the New Testament Jesus simplifies all that HE IS in one word... LOVE. I know that is simple.

He understands us better than anyone, so, understanding our nature, he brought it down in a bite size piece for us to grasp.

When we act in LOVE, it is impossible to judge, be hurtful or harmful, be self-absorbed... LOVE enables us to embrace, to understand, to extend grace and mercy. It allows us to listen, to learn, to speak with gentleness and kindness, and to extend a helping hand.

LOVE covers all things.

Above all, love each other deeply, because love covers a multitude of sins...

1 Peter 4:8

Do to others as you would have them do to you. If you love those who love you, what credit is that to you? Even sinners love those who love them.

Luke 6:31 - 32

The entire Law is fulfilled in a single word: Love your neighbor as yourself. If you keep on biting and devouring each other, watch out, or you will be consumed by each other.

Galatians 5:14 – 15

If I speak in the tongues of men and of angels, but have not love, I am only a ringing gong or a clanging cymbal. If I have the gift of prophecy and can fathom all mysteries and all knowledge, and if I have absolute faith so as to move mountains, but have not love, I am nothing. If I give all I possess to the poor and exult in the surrender of my body, but have not love, I gain nothing. Love is patient, love is kind. It does not envy, it does not boast, it is not proud. It is not rude, it is not self-seeking, it is not easily angered, it keeps no account of wrongs. Love takes no pleasure in evil but rejoices in the truth. It bears all things, believes all things, hopes all things, endures all things. Love never fails. But where there are prophecies, they will cease; where there are tongues, they will be restrained; where there is knowledge, it will be dismissed. For we know in part and we prophesy in part, but when the perfect comes, the partial passes away. When I was a child, I talked like a child, I thought like a child, I reasoned like a child. When I became a man, I set aside childish ways. Now we see but a dim reflection as in a mirror; then we shall see face to face. Now I know in part; then I shall know fully, even as I am fully known. And now these three remain: faith, hope, and love; but the greatest of these is love.

1 Corinthians 13

So, there it is. **LOVE.** Powerful, mighty, simplistic and some days a struggle. We, as humans, are flawed. Although it should be a goal for us on a daily basis, we will sometimes fail. But God's love for us is perfect and He knows our imperfection, so we keep fighting the good fight. And when it is hard to love others, we ask God to shape our words, **or our silence.** We ask God to intervene for us. We ask God to guide us and we surround ourselves in His love.

We read his word. We pray. We reflect on how we would like to be and work toward that. We ask for forgiveness when we fail, not only from God but from those persons whom we have wronged.

We do not cloud ourselves with the world and its thoughts, but shroud ourselves in God's grace and love, and EXTEND that to others. That is how they will see *His* face. That is how they will see and feel *His* love. That is how they will come to know *Him*, through you.

JUDGMENT AND **LOVE CANNOT** OCCUPY THE SAME SPACE.

To be the BOLD GOOD, we cannot offend through judgement. Judgment is NOT ours. To be the BOLD GOOD we stand for Jesus Christ. We become LOVE, because HE loved us. We smile when we are confronted with negativity. With a loving heart we extend a kind gesture to those who have just ticked us off in the store or in traffic and remind ourselves that perhaps their actions are the result of something more that we know nothing about. To see a change in the world, we must first be the change.

So, when we read that social post, we have a choice. We can either be silent or we can, in LOVE, without judgement, through prayer, respond in a way that will exemplify Christ.

If Jesus wouldn't post it, neither should we.

REFLECTION:

I challenge you to pray today for God to show you opportunity to Love, to extend Grace, to be the Jesus others will see. I challenge you to look for it, because if you ask, hold on, God will meet you there. When you see it, stop, pray, and allow God to use you and work through you.

Reflect on the occurrence. Write down your experience. Talk to God about the experience. You might handle it beautifully, or need a little assistance and some practice, that is ok. But be BOLD. Do NOT be afraid to show the LOVE of our Lord Jesus Christ.

FIVE

Be There

Making your ear attentive to wisdom and inclining your heart to understanding;

Proverbs 2:2

OVERVIEW
Be in the present.

Turn down the sound to the outside world and turn up the radar to detect the need around you.

Years ago, in a *'FISH'* training, I learned a valuable lesson.

BE PRESENT, WHEREVER YOU ARE.

What does that *really* mean? Well in this time of mobile phones, PlayStations, travel ball and distractions, it is often that our plates are so full that we are distracted frequently... and easily. Not to mention, just the allure of the blue light on the mobile, grabs our attention, for 'something to do' instead of looking at the world around us.

Hailing from the technology industry, I have often been known to gravitate toward the latest technology of... anything. But during this *'FISH'* training, what I learned was, I needed to be MORE PRESENT. How? How can I *be more* here than I already am? But looking, looking into the eyes of the person I am talking to, turning my shoulders toward them so that they can see I am there, with them, in the moment, taking time to really listen to them. Responding to what they are saying, asking clarifying questions for greater insight. Allowing them to speak about whatever it is they have on their mind and heart.

This is most important with my children. We have such a short amount of time with them, and if you have split households, you have even less. So, time becomes immensely valuable.

From the time our children are born til the day they turn 18, we have 936 weekends with them. Now, obviously they don't spend all that time with us. They have events, they go out with friends, retreats, etc. By the time they are a freshman in high school, we only have 208 left. And by the time they start their Senior year, we are down to only 36. It goes by very quickly. Unfortunately, there is a lot to compete with during this time.

I have made conscience effort over the last few years to 'be there' when I am speaking with someone. Making sure that, even if it is just for 5 min. that when I am speaking with them, that I am actively listening, looking, and responding. Do I successfully do this all the time? NOPE! But I can keep trying. People need to feel your interest. They need to know you are there. They need to understand that you are vested in them, and a great way to do that is to BE THERE, when you *are* there. Once again, this is a practice. If we are caught up in judgement of ourselves or others, we might miss the few opportunities we are actually given.

REFLECTION:

I challenge you to pray today for God to show you opportunity to Love, to extend grace, and to BE PRESENT at every personal interaction.

SIX

The Gospel According to you? Or God?

If anyone thinks he is religious and does not bridle his tongue but deceives his heart, this person's religion is worthless. Religion that is pure and undefiled before God, the Father, is this: to visit orphans and widows in their affliction, and to keep oneself unstained from the world.

James 1:26-27

OVERVIEW:
Don't get side tracked from God's actual word. Know it. Man can throw terms and ideas around that seem sound but have no scriptural basis.

Let's face it, there are lots of verses of scripture. It is difficult to know them all. Additionally, as I have watched and listened to my husband learn Greek, I have also learned that sometimes the way the scripture was originally taught to me, might not exactly have been the way it was originally written, or it might have only been taught to me partially. There are lots of things we say, that have been adopted from southern mom's tales, African Proverbs, Buddhist Proverbs, Irish Proverbs, and many others. They sound biblical, but they aren't. A few years ago, I had the privilege of sitting through *Half Truths*, by Adam Hamilton. If you haven't read this book or watched the videos I strongly recommend it.

In this work he had several things that we commonly say, that don't show up in the bible. The essence of what is said, might be there, or it might not. For example,

GOD WON'T GIVE YOU MORE THAN YOU CAN HANDLE.

I hate to say it, but **HE WILL.**

God will give you more than you can handle.

BECAUSE, GOD doesn't want YOU to handle it. HE wants you to draw closer to HIM and hand it over to HIM.

God will allow us to make bad decisions. God will allow us to go through valleys to shape us and stretch us so that we can grow closer to him and be more fitting for the road he has prepared for us. Is having Faith and Trust easy? No, that is why He says,

"Truly I tell you, if you have faith as small as a mustard seed, you can say to this mountain, "move from here to there,' and it will move. Nothing will be impossible for you.:
Mathew 17:20

A mustard seed is pretty small. God knows us. He knows our humanity. He created us. He isn't surprised when we doubt. He isn't surprised when we try to take back control. He just asks for a small amount of faith, because He knows sometimes that is all we can muster... He will do the rest, in His time, in His way, to fit His will for us. His plan for us is bigger than anything we could ever imagine.

FINALLY, know what *is* said. Spend time in the written word of God; not so much in the written word of man. Paul writes some of my favorite scripture. I find it inspiring. Sometimes course correcting. 'PUT ON THE FULL ARMOR OF GOD.' The battles in this world are far beyond what we can see. When we look at our children we want to prepare them for this world. We want to make sure that they have what ever it is that they need when they need it and GOD is no different when it comes to us. He wants to prepare us. He has set His word before us to show us the way.

Finally, be strong in the Lord and in the strength of his might. Put on the whole armor of God, that you may be able to stand against the schemes of the devil. For we do not wrestle against flesh and blood, but against the rulers, against the authorities, against the cosmic powers over this present darkness, against the spiritual forces of evil in the heavenly places. Therefore, take up the whole armor of God, that you may be able to withstand in the evil day, and having done all, to stand firm. Stand therefore, having fastened on the belt of truth, and having put on the breastplate of righteousness, ...
Ephesians 6:10-18

Know the difference between the gospel according to man and the gospel according to God. Only then can we have those Bold Good, loving conversations with those who are searching to meet Him face to face.

REFLECTION:

I challenge to seek God's word. Know the difference between the Gospel According to Man, and the Gospel According to God.

SEVEN

Careful HOW You Say It

For the anger of man does not produce the righteousness of God.

James 1:20

**OVERVIEW:
Right in the WRONG voice, is still wrong.**

Wow, those words written there, right above this line say it all, don't they? Right in the WRONG voice, is still wrong. That rings so true in today's confrontational society.

Recently a former colleague of mine posted a video on a social media channel. The video was from the 50's, it was of two women discussing their opposite perspectives on a topic. Now the topic is really of no matter; but HOW they discussed it was. Each woman, with poise, gentleness, kindness, and armed with their facts, presented their cases with true grit and grace. I was amazed. I was also a bit disappointed at how far we have come in our society that difference of opinions often means altercations, anger, and lack of grace with our grit.

I was once told MANY years ago, that

'He who shows anger in an argument first, loses.'

I don't like to lose; but when we show anger, we lose a bit of self-control. We say things we don't mean. We say them in ways we don't mean, and this has a lasting effect on a relationship. It chips away at the foundation. So, does it matter that you are right, if by being right you separate yourself from growth of a relationship, or from a loved one, or from a child, or from an opportunity?

Right in the **WRONG** voice, is still wrong.

This statement was said to me one day in the office by someone whom I respect. It was a situation where I was totally frustrated, and I, not in actual words, but in body language and temper, responded in such a way, that this was his response to me. It has stuck with me ever since. Anger is not productive. It is an inhibitor. It is not our friend...ever. Our human nature produces anger, so to control it we need to practice controlling it. Anyone can get angry. Anyone can lose their temper. But as we walk in the footsteps of Christ, we truly should not want to be just anyone. We should want to be seen as 'different'. We should want someone to notice our control, our love, our present-ness, our difference.

REFLECTION:

I challenge you to pray today for God work with you to control your anger. To speak in the RIGHT voice with the RIGHT words. We will not succeed every time, but with practice we will get better.

Made in the USA
Middletown, DE
31 May 2024